Golden Treasures

As Good as Gold: Carats of Wisdom From the Bible

A BARBOUR BOOK

Published by **Barbour and Company, Inc.**
P.O. Box 719
Uhrichsville, Ohio 44683

Typeset by Typetronix, Fort Myers, FL

ISBN 1-55748-348-5

Printed in the United States of America

1 2 3 4 5 / 98 97 96 95 94 93

Introduction

Golden Treasures is a special selection of inspirational writings and selected Scripture quotations from the newspaper columns of Herschel B. Dean.

Syndicated in over 500 newspapers as "Bible Digest," Reverend Dean's column of practical wisdom and Bible insight generated scores of testimonials.

Reverend Dean is no longer with us, but his words still shine brightly today, encouraging believers everywhere to follow the Light of the world!

"For God so loved the world, that he gave his only begotten Son, that whosoever believeth in him should not perish, but have everlasting life."

JOHN 3:16

If this was the only word we had from God, it would be enough. Put your name in the middle of it and get ready for excitement now and eternal life forever. Thanks, Father, You did it. We believe it.

WORDS OF ASSURANCE

"And Hezekiah received the letter of the hand of the messengers, and read it: and Hezekiah went up into the house of the Lord, and spread it before the Lord."

2 KINGS 19:14

We should be as wise with the burdens of life! Take them before the Lord and leave them there, before they take us under. "He careth for you."

"For I am with thee, and no man shall set on thee to hurt thee: for I have much people in this city."

Acts 18:10

In your darkest hour, remember that He who holds the whole world in the palm of His hand is watching and is able to deliver. "For he shall give his angels charge over thee, to keep thee in all thy ways."

"And he prayed again, and the heaven gave rain, and the earth brought forth her fruit."

JAMES 5:18

Here is the story of a man who, through faith and prayer, opened up Heaven. He is not in a class by himself. "These signs shall follow them that believe." Heaven will still open to those who approach it on the Lord's terms. "If ye shall ask anything in my name, I will do it."

"Because thou hast made the Lord, which is my refuge, even the most High, thy habitation; There shall no evil befall thee, neither shall any plague come nigh thy dwelling."

Psalm 91:9, 10

Every believer has the right to claim this promise and live with confidence that God will keep His Word as we embrace the condition.

"Commit thy way unto the Lord; trust also in him; and he shall bring it to pass."

PSALM 37:5

God hears and remembers well. Simply turn it over to Him once, and see what happens.

"The Lord is my light and my salvation; whom shall I fear? the Lord is the strength of my life; of whom shall I be afraid?"

PSALM 27:1

The man who walks with God doesn't have to run from anything. "Fear thou not; for I am with thee."

"... Death is swallowed up in victory. O death, where is thy sting? O grave, where is thy victory?"

1 CORINTHIANS 15:54, 55

Death is not a dead end but a doorway. Jesus said, "He that believeth on me, though he were dead, yet shall he live."

"He answered and said, Lo, I see four men loose, walking in the midst of the fire, and they have no hurt; and the form of the fourth is like the Son of God."

DANIEL 3:25

In every fiery trial of life, the child of God can expect the presence of the Saviour to see him through.

"Thy word is a lamp unto my feet, and a light unto my path."

PSALM 119:105

The Word of the Lord was meant to be used by men in travel from earth to Heaven. Perhaps the reason we have run into so many dark and gloomy roads along the way is because we have not recognized it.

"And Jesus answered him, saying, It is written, That man shall not live by bread alone, but by every word of God."

LUKE 4:4

A life dependent only on the physical and material is in for some lean times . . . but if the Spiritual intake of His Word has equal time with the physical, we can count on some strong bodies and great Christians.

". . . thy word is truth."

JOHN 17:17

Trust the word of man and you get what man can do. Trust the Word of God and you get what God has promised. He is able to do the exceeding and the abundant above all that we can ask or think.

"For ever, O Lord, thy word is settled in heaven."

PSALM 119:89

His Word is everlasting and never failing. We ought to give more heed to it.

"Whoso despiseth the word shall be destroyed: but he that feareth the commandment shall be rewarded."

PROVERBS 13:13

Respect His Word. Someday you will be judged by it. Use it today as a release of God's power. "The words that I speak unto you, they are spirit, and they are life."

"Keep therefore the words of this covenant, and do them, that ye may prosper in all that ye do."

DEUTERONOMY 29:9

Far from being a dry book, the Bible is a guide to all that we have dreamed of. Read a little of it every day and long after you have read, it will be back to bless you. "Thy word have I hid in mine heart, that I might not sin against thee."

"Yea, though I walk through the valley of the shadow of death, I will fear no evil: for thou art with me; thy rod and thy staff they comfort me."

PSALM 23:4

The man who has put his faith in God will not be afraid of the future. "Have faith in God."

"And Simon answering said unto him, Master, we have toiled all the night, and have taken nothing: nevertheless at thy word I will let down the net. And when they had this done, they inclosed a great multitude of fishes: and their net brake."

LUKE 5:5, 6

Jesus didn't go to where the fish were necessarily, but to where the faith was. He will honor our faith and obedience.

FAITH

" . . . Lord, if it be thou, bid me come unto thee on the water . . . he walked on the water, to go to Jesus."

MATTHEW 14:28, 29

When we step out on faith, the Lord will give us something to stand on. "Faith is the victory that overcomes the world." "Only believe."

"For verily I say unto you, That whosoever shall say unto this mountain, Be thou removed, and be thou cast into the sea; and shall not doubt in his heart, but shall believe that those things which he saith shall come to pass; he shall have whatsoever he saith."

MARK 11:23

Do what Jesus said. Speak to your mountains. They have done the talking long enough. "For with God nothing shall be impossible."

"By faith the walls of Jericho fell down, after they were compassed about seven days."

Hᴇʙʀᴇᴡs 11:30

There is no wall thick enough or armed enough to stand against one seed of faith. On with the march. Faith, praise, power and obedience will see the walls down and the windows of Heaven open. Praise God!

"And Jesus said unto them, Because of your unbelief: for verily I say unto you, If ye have faith as a grain of mustard seed, ye shall say unto this mountain, Remove hence to yonder place; and it shall remove; and nothing shall be impossible unto you."

MATTHEW 17:20

Take another look at this and never again make little of your faith, no matter how small it may look to you. It is mountain moving. Use it and a miracle is in the making.

FAITH

"For with God nothing shall be impossible."

LUKE 1:37

What the world needs is more mustard seed faith to remove manmade mountains. "According to your faith, so be it unto you."

FAITH

"By faith Abraham, when he was called to go out into a place which he should after receive for an inheritance, obeyed; and he went out, not knowing whither he went."

HEBREWS 11:8

If we take the first step of faith, it won't be too long until we see that we are not alone. "I will never leave thee nor forsake thee." The big word is obey. The big fact is that He loves us and has plans for our lives.

"For how shall I go up to my father, and the lad be not with me?"

GENESIS 44:34

In our great anxiety to see that our children won't miss anything, we should be super-careful that they don't miss the spiritual. Lead them to God, and take them to church. Forever you will be glad.

"Now there stood by the cross of Jesus his mother . . ."
JOHN 19:25

"Mother's prayers have followed you!" If she is still with you and you can't see her in person, whatever it costs, call and express your love to her. I wish I had the privilege.

"And they said, Believe on the Lord Jesus Christ, and thou shalt be saved, and thy house."

Acts 16:31

Pray on! Believe for the whole house Father, I join with them in believing for their whole family. Save them by Thy grace, in Jesus' name. Amen.

"And all thy children shall be taught of the Lord; and great shall be the peace of thy children."

ISAIAH 54:13

Get the child to God and to the Lord's house while there is time. You can be sure that the enemy of all that is good and wholesome will be after them. Don't squander the privilege to worship. Millions before and multitudes now would love the opportunity.

"And they with whom precious stones were found gave them to the treasure of the house of the Lord . . ."

1 CHRONICLES 29:8

Giving God the leftovers didn't originate with Old Testament giving habits. If they tithed before Christ came, surely we should at least do as much. Quit tipping God and start tithing. "God loves a cheerful giver."

"And all the tithe of the land, whether of the seed of the land, or of the fruit of the tree, is the Lord's: it is holy unto the Lord."

LEVITICUS 27:30

Is ten percent of what He has given you too much to ask for the work that you claim, as a Christian, to be the most important thing on earth? Try tithing for one month and see the miracle of it all.

"And he called unto him his disciples, and saith unto them, Verily I say unto you, That this poor widow hath cast more in, than all they which have cast into the treasury."

MARK 12:43

This has always been true on the average. The poor people support the work of God, while the wealthy give a few crumbs for the cause of Christ while off in search of some project to exalt their own name above His. Why don't you call your pastor and ask what you can do to really make your means count?

"And this stone, which I have set for a pillar, shall be God's house: and of all that thou shalt give me I will surely give the tenth unto thee."

GENESIS 28:22

The faith of every believer ought to be shared by systematic giving and some supernatural living. The more you give, the more you will want to give, and the more you will have to give.

"Withhold not good from them to whom it is due, when it is in the power of thine hand to do it. Say not unto thy neighbour, Go, and come again, and tomorrow I will give; when thou hast it by thee."

PROVERBS 3:27, 28

We can get so busy talking spiritual that we neglect to do something practical! The Church could use more Christians in work clothes. Share with some needy person today.

"For I was an hungred, and ye gave me no meat: I was thirsty, and ye gave me no drink: I was a stranger, and ye took me not in: naked, and ye clothed me not: sick, and in prison, and ye visited me not."

MATTHEW 25:42, 43

Jesus often appears in the form of neglected and little people, to see if we will do even the simple things as proof of our love and loyalty to Him personally.

"Lay not up for yourselves treasures upon earth, where moth and rust doth corrupt, and where thieves break through and steal: But lay up for yourselves treasures in heaven, where neither moth nor rust doth corrupt; and where thieves do not break through nor steal."

MATTHEW 6:19, 20

One of the greatest drawbacks to Christianity is the Christian's savings account. The rainy day is here. Give what you can, while you can, to share the Gospel of Christ. Forever, you will be glad.

"I have showed you all things, how that so labouring ye ought to support the weak, and to remember the words of the Lord Jesus, how he said, It is more blessed to give than to receive."

Acts 20:35

This may not fit in with our thinking, but it fits in with His planning. Do some giving and watch God.

"For God so loved the world, that he gave his only begotten Son, that whosoever believeth in him should not perish, but have everlasting life."

JOHN 3:16

God's love is big enough to cover the world and yet individual enough so that the least of us are included.

"He that spared not his own Son, but delivered him up for us all, how shall he not with him also freely give us all things?"

ROMANS 8:32

Believe big! What you are asking is nothing compared to what He has already given. "Is any thing too hard for the Lord?"

GOD'S LOVE

"The Lord is gracious, and full of compassion . . . and of great mercy."

PSALM 145:8

He who said, "I have compassion on the multitude" is still interested in solving even the smallest problem. Earth has no sorrow that Heaven cannot heal.

"I will say of the Lord, He is my refuge and my fortress: my God; in him will I trust."

PSALM 91:2

He is both a place to hide and abide. Come in out of the storm and strife of life regularly and meet with your Maker. You will be better equipped to face the world and do His work.

GOD'S LOVE

"And I will give thee the treasures of darkness, and hidden riches of secret places, that thou mayest know that I, the Lord, which call thee by thy name, am the God of Israel."

ISAIAH 45:3

"No good thing will he withhold from them that walk uprightly." Father, guide Your children into all the prosperity that You planned for us spiritually and physically and give us a generous spirit to go with it. In Jesus' dear name. Amen.

"But God commendeth his love toward us, in that, while we were yet sinners, Christ died for us."

ROMANS 5:8

Long before it was decided which way you were going, Jesus went to the cross to assure you of the abundant and eternal life. "He that believeth on the Son hath everlasting life: and he that believeth not the Son shall not see life . . ."

"Jesus answered and said unto him, If a man love me, he will keep my words: and my Father will love him, and we will come unto him, and make our abode with him."

JOHN 14:23

Behold the reward in the keeping of His Word! "We will come unto him, and make our abode with him." What living . . . what love! "Greater is he that is in you than he that is in the world."

"And he will love thee, and bless thee, and multiply thee: he will also bless the fruit of thy womb, and the fruit of thy land, thy corn, and thy wine, and thine oil, the increase of thy kine, and the flocks of thy sheep, in the land which he sware unto thy fathers to give thee."

DEUTERONOMY 7:13

What a promise! What a fulfillment! "My word shall not return unto me void."

"And as ye would that men should do to you, do ye also to them likewise."

LUKE 6:31

Here is the beginning of the new world you have always wanted to create.

"Enter not into the path of the wicked, and go not in the way of evil men."

PROVERBS 4:14

Don't ask for trouble by placing yourself in the path of the evildoer. We are in the world, but we don't have to be of it. Follow God's way as He says, "This is the way, walk ye in it."

"Commit thy way unto the Lord; trust also in him; and he shall bring it to pass."

PSALM 37:5

The reason that the Lord doesn't bring a lot of things to pass is because He can't get past us. Move over and let God take the lead. "His ways are not our ways."

"As ye have therefore received Christ Jesus the Lord, so walk ye in him."

COLOSSIANS 2:6

It is as important to keep Him in our walk as it is to keep Him in our worship. A sermon in shoes stands out.

"Again, the kingdom of heaven is like unto a merchant man, seeking goodly pearls: Who, when he had found one pearl of great price, went and sold all that he had, and bought it."

MATTHEW 13:45, 46

This is a lesson in majoring in main things. Put all that you have and all that you are in the one and only thing that really counts.

"Judge not, and ye shall not be judged: condemn not, and ye shall not be condemned: forgive, and ye shall be forgiven."

LUKE 6:37

Before we can be cleansed of our own faults, we must have everything in the clear with our neighbor. "If ye forgive not, neither will your heavenly Father forgive you."

"Fret not thyself because of evildoers, neither be thou envious against the workers of iniquity."

PSALM 37:1

It is easy to get so wrapped up in condemning evil that we grow negligent in doing good.

"Therefore I say unto you, Take no thought for your life, what ye shall eat, or what ye shall drink; nor yet for your body, what ye shall put on. Is not the life more than meat, and the body than raiment?"

MATTHEW 6:25

Here is where we put the most emphasis and Jesus said where we should put the least. "But seek ye first the kingdom of God, and his righteousness; and all these things shall be added unto you."

"But ye shall receive power, after that the Holy Ghost is come upon you: and ye shall be witnesses unto me both in Jerusalem, and in all Judea, and in Samaria, and unto the uttermost part of the earth."

ACTS 1:8

Too long have we tried to produce on our own power and have discovered that we have the wrong connection and the lines were down. We must be filled with the Spirit or be content with human frustration.

"And it shall come to pass afterward, that I will pour out my spirit upon all flesh; and your sons and your daughters shall prophesy, your old men shall dream dreams, your young men shall see visions: And also upon the servants and upon the handmaids in those days will I pour out my spirit ."

JOEL 2:28, 29

We can see the evidence of that day in our time and, though many cannot understand it, none of us can deny it. Holy Spirit, breathe on us and empower us to evangelize the world in our time. In Jesus' name, Amen.

"... Not by might, nor by power, but by my spirit, saith the Lord of Hosts."

ZECHARIAH 4:6

We are guilty of depending on our own working and wisdom, and not depending upon the Holy Spirit and His power. If we would be happy in our Christian experience, we need to relieve ourselves of the strain of so many works of our own and submit all to the guidance of the Holy Spirit.

"Quench not the Spirit."

1 THESSALONIANS 5:19

There is no substitute for the Spirit of God. "If any man have not the Spirit of God, he is none of his."

"But the fruit of the Spirit is love, joy, peace, longsuffering, gentleness, goodness, faith, Meekness, temperance: against such there is no law."

GALATIANS 5:22, 23

Here are the fruits of the Spirit, the outgrowth of the indwelling of His great presence. "By this shall all men know that ye are my disciples, if ye have love one to another."

"For to one is given by the Spirit the word of wisdom; to another the word of knowledge by the same Spirit; . . . To another the working of miracles; to another prophecy; to another discerning of spirits; to another divers kinds of tongues; to another the interpretation of tongues."

1 CORINTHIANS 12:8, 10

Here are the gifts of the Spirit, given to be shared as starters for all else that God has for those who open up themselves to be used of Him.

"... This is my beloved Son, in whom I am well pleased."

MATTHEW 3:17

Jesus came into the world, lived under great hardships and died on the cross to satisfy His Father. What have you done to please Him?

"Jesus saith unto him, I am the way, the truth, and the life: no man cometh unto the Father but by me."

JOHN 14:6

Jesus is the way to eternal life and any detour that we make for ourselves will only lead to a dead end. Ask Him boldly now to bless you with His presence and He will. "Behold, I stand at the door and knock: if any man will open the door, I will come in."

"Jesus said unto her, I am the resurrection, and the life: he that believeth in me, though he were dead, yet shall he live."

JOHN 11:25

Jesus conquered death and claims the same victory for all who confess Him as Saviour. "O death, where is thy sting? O grave, where is thy victory?"

". . . his name shall be called Wonderful, Counsellor, The mighty God, The everlasting Father, The Prince of Peace."

ISAIAH 9:6

He has been true to His name and true to His Word. He is qualified to help you in every area of life. Trust Him today!

"And he saith unto them, Why are ye fearful, O ye of little faith? Then he arose, and rebuked the winds and the sea; and there was a great calm."

MATTHEW 8:26

No man can afford to face the storms of life without the Divine Captain. His presence alone brings calmness, confidence, and courage.

"In whom we have redemption through his blood, even the forgiveness of sins."

COLOSSIANS 1:14

Nothing less and nothing more can settle the sin question in our lives. The blood of Jesus Christ, God's Son, cleanseth us from all sins. The application is in acknowledging that He died for us and we cannot really live without Him.

"And Ruth said, Intreat me not to leave thee, or to return from following after thee: for whither thou goest, I will go; and where thou lodgest, I will lodge: thy people shall be my people, and thy God my God."

RUTH 1:16

Love is a mysterious force imparted by God the Father and gloriously shared by His creatures to degrees beyond human comprehension and reason. No wonder the Lord said of the first Christians, "By this shall all men know that ye are my disciples, if ye have love one to another."

"But I say unto you, Love your enemies, bless them that curse you, do good to them that hate you, and pray for them which despitefully use you, and persecute you."

MATTHEW 5:44

If the spirit of Christ surfaces at this point in your life, you will know that you have done more than joined a church. All men will know that "Ye are my disciples, if ye have love one to another."

LOVE

"Master, which is the great commandment in the law? Jesus said unto him, Thou shalt love the Lord thy God with all thy heart, and with all thy soul, and with all thy mind. This is the first and great commandment. And the second is like unto it, Thou shalt love thy neighbour as thyself."

MATTHEW 22:36-39

The reason the world is in trouble today is because we have made so little over the great commandment. "Love covers a multitude of sins."

LOVE

"For God so loved the world, that he gave his only begotten Son, that whosoever believeth in him should not perish, but have everlasting life."

JOHN 3:16

God's love is big enough to cover the world and, yet, individual enough so that the least of us are included.

LOVE

"This is my commandment, That ye love one another, as I have loved you."

JOHN 15:12

All the world's problems through Jesus will be settled at this point or not at all. "Now abideth faith, hope, love; the greatest of these is love."

LOVE

"I will love thee, O Lord, my strength."

PSALM 18:1

If the love of God is in our hearts, we will show it in our lives. "By this shall all men know that ye are my disciples, if ye have love one to another."

"Whether therefore ye eat, or drink, or whatsoever ye do, do all to the glory of God."

1 CORINTHIANS 10:31

Here is the argument settler. If you can't do a thing in accordance with His Word and will, don't do it. "Not my will, but thine, be done."

"... All that the Lord hath said will we do, and be obedient."
Exodus 24:7

God's paths are clear. It is our dull hearing that gets us into trouble. "Obedience is better than sacrifice." "We ought to obey God rather than man."

"Then the king commanded, and they brought Daniel, and cast him into the den of lions. Now the king spake and said unto Daniel, Thy God whom thou servest continually, he will deliver thee."

DANIEL 6:16

Our job is dedication—His is deliverance. If we give attention to doing His will, the Lord is good enough to give us even beyond what we ask.

"His lord said unto him, Well done, thou good and faithful servant: thou hast been faithful over a few things, I will make thee ruler over many things: enter thou into the joy of thy lord."

MATTHEW 25:21

Contrary to what we sometimes think we will be rewarded not for our success but on the basis of our faithfulness. "Be thou faithful unto death, and I will give thee a crown of life."

"The impotent man answered him, Sir, I have no man, when the water is troubled, to put me into the pool: but while I am coming, another steppeth down before me. Jesus saith unto him, Rise, take up thy bed, and walk."

JOHN 5:7, 8

This is a story of a man who allowed Jesus to come into his life and exchange his explanation into an experience that put him on his feet. If you are looking for a real happening in your life, He is the one who can do it.

"But one thing is needful."

LUKE 10:42

There is one thing that is truly necessary in life, and that is to have Christ. There are many things in this life that are out of reach, but here is man's greatest need within the reach of all.

"Behold, I am the Lord, the God of all flesh: is there any thing too hard for me?"

JEREMIAH 32:27

Weigh your problem over against His promise . . . and believe for the answer! "All things are possible to him that believeth." "All power is given unto me in heaven and in earth."

But my God shall supply all your need according to his riches in glory by Christ Jesus."

PHILIPPIANS 4:19

If you belong to God, you are entitled to what He has. He invites you to ask for it. "Ask what ye will."

"But seek ye first the kingdom of God, and his righteousness; and all these things shall be added unto you."

MATTHEW 6:33

It seems like Jesus is saying that once our priorities are in order, answers to our prayers will be automatic.

"Be not ye therefore like unto them: for your Father knoweth what things ye have need of, before ye ask him."
MATTHEW 6:8

Take time to thank Him for the needs met upon request, but also for the many met without request. "But my God shall supply all your need according to his riches in glory by Christ Jesus."

"I am the good shepherd: the good shepherd giveth his life for the sheep."

JOHN 10:11

On the cross, Jesus identified Himself with every sin, struggle and crisis of life. In this moment, receive that as a cure for every problem and go free forever. Father, I ask for salvation for everyone and liberation from every hurt and habit that may be harassing them. In Jesus' name, Amen.

"Come unto me, all ye that labour and are heavy laden, and I will give you rest."

MATTHEW 11:28

Think of all the peace we forfeit because we will not act on this promise. Father, we come with our burdens and we believe You for miracles, in Jesus' name. Amen, and thank You.

"Happy is that people, that is in such a case: yea, happy is that people, whose God is the Lord."

PSALM 144:15

Here is where happiness is! Isn't it strange that we have searched for it in so many other things and places? Father, forgive us, in Jesus' name. Amen.

"Therefore being justified by faith, we have peace with God through our Lord Jesus Christ."

ROMANS 5:1

There is no real peace inside, outside of Christ. He gives the peace that passeth all understanding. Peace that the world cannot give or take away.

"Peace I leave with you, my peace I give unto you: not as the world giveth, give I unto you. Let not your heart be troubled, neither let it be afraid."

JOHN 14:27

The peace that counts is found at an altar of prayer, not at a table. Let's get back to the Bible . . . and God.

"Yet I will rejoice in the Lord, I will joy in the God of my salvation."

HABAKKUK 3:18

There are good times in God's service. He planned it that way. Give Him praise. "Rejoice in the Lord alway: and again I say, Rejoice." Not only prayer but praise is mountain moving.

"Praise ye the Lord. Praise God in his sanctuary: praise him in the firmament of his power."

PSALM 150:1

When was the last time you heard praise in the sanctuary —that is to God! Praise ye the Lord. "Let everything that hath breath praise the Lord."

"Praise the Lord; for the Lord is good: sing praises unto his name; for it is pleasant."

PSALM 135:3

Praise should be a definite part of our life every day. It probably would surprise us if we knew how much answered prayer depends on our attitude of praise to God. "Be thankful unto him, and bless his name."

"Fear not, O land; be glad and rejoice: for the Lord will do great things."

JOEL 2:21

So many times the victory is in the rejoicing rather than in the pleading. Thank Him in advance now; and acknowledge that He is able to do above and beyond what you can ask or think.

"And one of them, when he saw that he was healed, turned back, and with a loud voice glorified God, And fell down on his face at his feet, giving him thanks: and he was a Samaritan."

LUKE 17:15, 16

We all go to Him in prayer, but how many times do we return to Him in thanks? And we hear a lot about prayer lists, but when was the last time you heard of a praise list? It is a good thing to give thanks unto the Lord.

PRAISING GOD

"This is the day which the Lord hath made; we will rejoice and be glad in it."

PSALM 118:24

He has made the day. Praising Him for it makes it better! From the rising of the sun to the going down thereof, His praise shall continually be in my mouth.

"And in that day shall ye say, Praise the Lord, call upon his name, declare his doings among the people, make mention that his name is exalted."

ISAIAH 12:4

Praise Him for what He has done, and in advance for what you expect Him to do. What a volume of praise would rise today if for one moment we would thank Him for past blessings. I praise Thee, oh God. Praise Father, Son, and Holy Ghost. Amen.

"For this cause I bow my knees unto the Father of our Lord Jesus Christ."

EPHESIANS 3:14

More bowing of the knees means less bowing to the world. You can go all the way to the top on your knees. Prayer is priceless. "Pray without ceasing."

"Confess your faults one to another, and pray one for another, that ye may be healed. The effectual fervent prayer of a righteous man availeth much."

JAMES 5:16

It is good to be pulling for someone, but much better to be praying for them. Right now, take a moment to lift a prayer for someone. It could mean the difference in their life here and their future in the hereafter.

"And all things, whatsoever ye shall ask in prayer, be-lieving, ye shall receive."

MATTHEW 21:22

Go up against your greatest problem with this simple prayer pattern and look for answers, for they are sure to come. Jesus said, ". . . I will do it."

PRAYER

"... one of his disciples said unto him, Lord, teach us to pray ..."

LUKE 11:1

It would seem that the closer a man is to the Lord, the more he sees his need of prayer. Prayer is a personal inventory of our spiritual needs and a private audience with Him "who sticketh closer than a brother."

PRAYER

"After this manner therefore pray ye: Our Father which art in heaven, Hallowed be thy name. Thy kingdom come. Thy will be done in earth, as it is in heaven. Give us this day our daily bread. And forgive us our debts, as we forgive our debtors. And lead us not into temptation, but deliver us from evil: For thine is the kingdom, and the power, and the glory, for ever. Amen."

MATTHEW 6:9-13

Don't try to analyze or sermonize on this prayer. Just gather up all your problems and simply, slowly, and reverently repeat it. Let it be a daily part of you. In it, you are going to God in the words and in the name of His Son. You are bound to get results.

"I love them that love me; and those that seek me early shall find me."

PROVERBS 8:17

What kind of priority does prayer have? "Seek ye first the kingdom of God, and his righteousness; and all these things shall be added unto you."

"Submit yourselves therefore to God. Resist the devil, and he will flee from you."

JAMES 4:7

Speak up to the devil in the name of Jesus. "Greater is he that is in you, than he that is in the world." Jesus said, "I am with you always."

"Jesus answered them, Verily, verily, I say unto you, Whosoever committeth sin is the servant of sin."

JOHN 8:34

Sin is a hard boss to work for. Long hours, broken hearts, worried minds, and a multitude of bitter memories are the products of the devil. "The wages of sin is death." Be no longer the servant of sin when there is complete release in Christ.

"Then saith Jesus unto him, Get thee hence, Satan: for it is written, Thou shalt worship the Lord thy God, and him only shalt thou serve. Then the devil leaveth him, and, behold, angels came and ministered unto him."

MATTHEW 4:10, 11

There is a liberation of our spirit that comes only from looking up to the Lord and speaking up to the devil. "Resist the devil and he will flee from you." We overcome by the "word of our testimony and the blood of the Lamb." Thank you, Lord, for the power of Your blood and the might of Your Word! Amen.

"Be not overcome of evil, but overcome evil with good."

ROMANS 12:21

Keep firing away with good. Someday evil will surrender. "A soft answer turneth away wrath."

"Neither is there salvation in any other: for there is none other name under heaven given among men, whereby we must be saved."

Acts 4:12

Contrary to what so many seem to believe, salvation is in neither the church nor a cause, but through Christ alone. Jesus said, "I am the way."

"Behold, I stand at the door, and knock: if any man hear my voice, and open the door, I will come in to him, and will sup with him, and he with me."

REVELATION 3:20

What if suddenly you felt the silence of the departure of His presence, never to return again? "My spirit will not always strive with man." Answer the door now, and invite Him into the living room, the place where you live, and let Him take over for life.

"For all have sinned, and come short of the glory of God."

ROMANS 3:23

No sinner is so bad but what he can find refuge in the goodness of God through Christ the Saviour. "Jesus saves."

SALVATION

"For by grace are ye saved through faith; and that not of yourselves: it is the gift of God."

EPHESIANS 2:8

No amount of work can save you, but just a little faith will write your name in the Book of Life. Scrap your plans and accept His plan of salvation.

"I said, Lord, be merciful unto me: heal my soul; for I have sinned against thee."

PSALM 41:4

Every man's soul very often stands in need of spiritual repair. The Great Physician, Christ Jesus, stands ready to do the job. He has never lost a patient.

"For by grace are ye saved through faith; and that not of yourselves: it is the gift of God: Not of works, lest any man should boast."

EPHESIANS 2:8, 9

No man works his way up to Heaven. Our eternal salvation is settled in the Saviour, not in the efforts of man.

"That if thou shalt confess with thy mouth the Lord Jesus, and shalt believe in thine heart that God hath raised him from the dead, thou shalt be saved."

ROMANS 10:9

The evidence of real Christian experience is a combination of what we feel in our hearts and what we say with our lives.

SALVATION

"Jesus answered and said unto him, Verily, verily, I say unto thee, Except a man be born again, he cannot see the kingdom of God."

JOHN 3:3

It is impossible for man to have a new life without a new birth. Being a Christian is a great deal more than joining a church and making resolutions. It is experiencing a regeneration through a crucified Redeemer.

"... him that cometh to me I will in no wise cast out."
JOHN 6:37

Every honest seeker in Christ will find his eternal salvation. Nothing shall separate us from the love of God.

"Come unto me, all ye that labour and are heavy laden, and I will give you rest. Take my yoke upon you, and learn of me; for I am meek and lowly in heart: and ye shall find rest unto your souls. For my yoke is easy, and my burden is light."

MATTHEW 11:28-30

You can't beat this invitation, but it's not going to be there forever. Today is the day of Salvation. You will never relive today. Make it a good one with God's help.

"I was glad when they said unto me, Let us go into the house of the Lord."

PSALM 122:1

You can tell those who love the Lord by the excuses they find to attend His House. You can also tell those who don't love Him so much by the excuses they seem to find to stay away from His House. Christ loved the Church, and gave Himself for it.

"He must increase, but I must decrease."

JOHN 3:30

The business of every Christian is to lift up the Saviour and play down self. The greatest problem of the Church is that we have not held Him up as the answer.

"Ye are the light of the world . . ."

MATTHEW 5:14

Not just the Church, not a select few, but each one in his own way that stands for the cause of Christianity. How much light have you been responsible for to dispense the gloom and doubt of a troubled soul yet in darkness?

"... Thou shalt worship the Lord thy God, and him only shalt thou serve."

MATTHEW 4:10

Strange and curious gods daily make their appearance in all of our lives to crowd out the true and living God. Let it be known that you are not for hire. It is a noble thing to be a real servant.

"For whosoever shall give you a cup of water to drink in my name, because ye belong to Christ, verily I say unto you, he shall not lose his reward."

MARK 9:41

Our attitude toward the little things are important.

"And Jesus said unto them, Come ye after me, and I will make you to become fishers of men."

MARK 1:17

If it has not been your happy privilege to point a soul to Christ, it matters little else what your achievements have been. There is no business like God's business.

".. . Here am I; send me."

ISAIAH 6:8

The greatest contribution is the gift of ourselves in the service of the Lord. A lot of big jobs are waiting to be filled by dedicated little people.

". . . Lord, what wilt thou have me to do? And the Lord said unto him, Arise, and go into the city, and it shall be told thee what thou must do."

Acts 9:6

God will take the willing worker, all-out for Christ, in preference to the wise ones who feel they have all the answers.

"Hath not my hand made all these things?"

ACTS 7:50

So little of our lives revolve around Him, who created us, and the world that we live in. So much depends on our attitude toward Him and what we do with the Saviour.

"Let all the earth fear the Lord: let all the inhabitants of the world stand in awe of him."

PSALM 33:8

We need but to look around us to know that there is a greater power above us. The need of the hour is for the created to have more respect for the Creator.

THE SOVEREIGNTY OF GOD

"I am the Lord: that is my name: and my glory will I not give to another, neither my praise to graven images."

ISAIAH 42:8

Love and appreciate others and even love yourself, but all the glory and the praise, plus the greatest of our love must go to Him. All that we are, have, or will be is because of Him. "He hath made us and not we ourselves." Oh God, our Heavenly Father, we praise You and give honor and glory to Your name. Thank You for Jesus and the Holy Spirit and Your Word. We praise You for abundant life here and eternal life in Heaven, through Jesus Christ, Your Son. Amen.

"And the Lord shall be king over all the earth: in that day shall there be one Lord, and his name one."

ZECHARIAH 14:9

The day will come when the One who made it all will rule over all. Blessed are those subjects who will already have made Him Lord of Lords and King of Kings.

"Therefore if any man be in Christ, he is a new creature: old things are passed away; behold, all things are become new."

2 Corinthians 5:17

Our meeting with Christ always makes the difference. We will know it, and so will others. "Let your light so shine before men, that they may see your good works, and glorify your Father which is in heaven."

"Jesus answered and said unto him, Verily, verily, I say unto thee, Except a man be born again, he cannot see the kingdom of God."

JOHN 3:3

The new birth is a lot more than a decision to do a little better. It is a departure of the old nature, giving way to new life in Christ. It becomes "Christ in you the hope of glory." Father, help us all to see how easy it is to receive Jesus, and yet how easy it is to pass Him by and lose eternal life forever.

". . . Behold, I make all things new . . ."

REVELATION 21:5

God has the power and is willing to give us a new start. If you are tired of the old life, then accept the new one that He has for you. "If any man be in Christ, he is a new creature: old things are passed away; behold, all things are become new."

"Come now, and let us reason together, saith the Lord: though your sins be as scarlet, they shall be as white as snow; though they be red like crimson, they shall be as wool."

ISAIAH 1:18

If an artist is able to take a piece of junk and make it into a thing of beauty, think of what the Lord can do with our lives turned over to Him. Let the Lord Redeemer recycle your life today. You will be glad with the results.

"That which is born of the flesh is flesh; and that which is born of the Spirit is spirit."

JOHN 3:6

Here is the heart of God in the interest of the souls of men. The next move is yours. Jesus said, "Come unto me . . . him that cometh to me I will in no wise cast out."

"Enter ye in at the strait gate: for wide is the gate, and broad is the way, that leadeth to destruction, and many there be which go in thereat: Because strait is the gate, and narrow is the way, which leadeth unto life, and few there be that find it."

MATTHEW 7:13, 14

Heaven is no walk-in or pushover. "Except a man be born again, he cannot see the kingdom of God."

"Now unto him that is able to keep you from falling, and to present you faultless before the presence of his glory with exceeding Joy."

JUDE 24

Don't worry about the carry-over of the old life once you have surrendered it to Him. "If any man be in Christ, he is a new creature." "Behold, I make all things new."

"For the Lord himself shall descend from heaven with a shout, with the voice of the archangel, and with the trump of God: and the dead in Christ shall rise first: Then we which are alive and remain shall be caught up together with them in the clouds to meet the Lord in the air: and so shall we ever be with the Lord."

1 Thessalonians 4:16, 17

What a beautiful picture of the future! But remember, there is no reunion without regeneration! "Except a man be born again, he cannot see the kingdom of God." You can take care of that in the next moment by turning from your sins and inviting Jesus into your heart.

"Nevertheless I have somewhat against thee, because thou hast left thy first love."

REVELATION 2:4

The Lord's message to the Church is simply to "come back" from our wanderings get off the religious routine bit, and get on with the message that man is a sinner and Jesus is the Saviour, and without Him there is no redemption. Only in this is there hope for the Church and help for the world.

"And Peter remembered the word of Jesus, which said unto him, Before the cock crow, thou shalt deny me thrice. And he went out, and wept bitterly."

MATTHEW 26:75

Tears have been the way back for many discouraged Christians who have warmed themselves by the enemy's fire. He will not turn thee away.

"He that hath no rule over his own spirit is like a city that is broken down, and without walls."

PROVERBS 25:28

It is so easy to lose control if Christ is not at the center of your life. "Let the Spirit of Christ reign in your heart."

"Neglect not the gift that is in thee . . ."

1 TIMOTHY 4:14

We need to develop our own God-given talents, instead of trying to duplicate what He has given to another.

TRUSTING GOD

"That thy trust may be in the Lord, I have made known to thee this day, even to thee. Have not I written to thee excellent things in counsels and knowledge."

PROVERBS 22:19, 20

Life's answers are lost to us because we keep leaning on our own understanding or taking the advice of those who are as much in the dark as we are. Read the Bible every day and apply it to your everyday need.

"Trust ye in the Lord for ever: for in the Lord JEHOVAH is everlasting strength."

Isaiah 26:4

Enlist your life in the service of the Lord forever. Don't worry about the "holding out," for in Him is "everlasting strength." "I will uphold thee with the right hand of my righteousness." "Have faith in God."

TRUSTING GOD

"But it is good for me to draw near to God: I have put my trust in the Lord God, that I may declare all thy works."

PSALM 73:28

Our greatest need is to be near to God. All else that is good and worthwhile will follow. "Draw nigh to God, and he will draw nigh to You."

"And the Lord shall help them, and deliver them: he shall deliver them from the wicked, and save them, because they trust in him."

PSALM 37:40

The Lord is in the deliverance business Special delivery! "Behold, I am the Lord, the God of all flesh: is there anything too hard for me?"

"For what shall it profit a man, if he shall gain the whole world, and lose his own soul? Or what shall a man give in exchange for his soul?"

MARK 8:36, 37

An eternity without God and the good things He has prepared is a terrible price to pay for having our own way over things that will soon pass away. "Seek ye first the kingdom of God, and his righteousness; and all these things shall be added unto you."

"Therefore be ye also ready: for in such an hour as ye think not the Son of man cometh."

MATTHEW 24:44

A person who is not ready to die is not ready to live. A person who is not ready to meet his Master in His second coming cannot fully appreciate the fact that He came the first time.

"I tell you, in that night there shall be two men in one bed; the one shall be taken, and the other shall be left. Two women shall be grinding together; the one shall be taken, and the other left. Two men shall be in the field; the one shall be taken, and the other left. And they answered and said unto him, Where, Lord? And he said unto them, Wheresoever the body is, thither will the eagles be gathered together."

LUKE 17:34-37

Here is a picture of the final day on earth of people who will probably have plans of what all they are going to do for the Lord, and others who were going to get right with the Lord. Do it now. "No man knoweth the day nor the hour when the Son of man cometh."

"Take ye heed, watch and pray: for ye know not when the time is."

MARK 13:33

Time is in God's hands. Talents are in our hands. We ought to use them wisely before time runs out. The time is short.

"But if from thence thou shalt seek the Lord thy God, thou shalt find him, if thou seek him with all thy heart and with all thy soul."

DEUTERONOMY 4:29

Whoever you are, and wherever you are along the road of life, if you get serious with God, you are going to see things you never dreamed possible. "Seek ye the Lord while he may be found . . . call ye upon him while he is near."

"I am the vine, ye are the branches: He that abideth in me, and I in him, the same bringeth forth much fruit: for without me ye can do nothing."

JOHN 15:5

Abiding in Him is even more productive than activity for Him. "Not by might, nor by power, but by my spirit, saith the Lord."

"Let the words of my mouth, and the meditation of my heart, be acceptable in thy sight, O Lord, my strength, and my redeemer."

PSALM 19:14

Not only what we talk about, but what we think about, is screened by the Lord. Is it acceptable to the Lord?

"And when forty years were expired, there appeared to him in the wilderness of mount Sina an angel of the Lord in a flame of fire in a bush."

ACTS 7:30

God is still speaking through unusual means, and many times through unknown people, to get His message across.

"For where two or three are gathered together in my name, there am I in the midst of them."

MATTHEW 18:20

Careful that you don't make light of a few believers gathered, unless you want to take the responsibility of counting the presence of the Saviour as nothing.

"But thanks be to God, which giveth us the victory through our Lord Jesus Christ."

1 CORINTHIANS 15:57

There is a victory in the valley with Him who gives us a passing gear and a rising gear. The Lord takes the pressure and struggle out of religion, and lets us know that there are good times in God's service. Too many of us are content in holding on to what we have, at the cost of overlooking what God has for us.

"And ye shall know the truth, and the truth shall make you free."

JOHN 8:32

It is the truth that turns us around and sets us free. "Jesus said, I am the way, the truth, and the life: no man cometh unto the Father, but by me." May this be the turning point and the liberation of multitudes in this moment, my Father, as they receive Your Son Jesus into their heart. In His name. Amen.

"I have no greater joy than to hear that my children walk in truth."

3 JOHN 4

Honest talk is good, if it is followed by honest walk. Truth is a terror to the unrighteous and a test to the righteous.

". . . The Lord is with you, while ye be with him; and if ye seek him, he will be found of you; but if ye forsake him, he will forsake you."

2 CHRONICLES 15:2

The Lord is not in hiding. He is as close as your call. Father, may multitudes meet You, today, in Jesus' name. Amen.